D1242370

SandCastle 1

Zoo Animals

Elephants

Carey Molter

ABDO
Publishing Company

3102

Center for children's books

Published by SandCastle™, an imprint of ABDO Publishing Company, 4940 Viking Drive, Edina, Minnesota 55435.

Printed in the United States.

Cover and interior photo credits: Corbis Images, Corel, Digital Stock, PhotoDisc.

Library of Congress Cataloging-in-Publication Data

Molter, Carey, 1973-
     Elephants / Carey Molter.
        p. cm. -- (Zoo animals)
     ISBN 1-57765-560-5
       1. Elephants--Juvenile literature. [Elephants.] I. Title

     QL737.P98 M64 2001
     599.67--dc21

                                     2001022007

The SandCastle concept, content, and reading method have been reviewed and approved by a national advisory board including literacy specialists, librarians, elementary school teachers, early childhood education professionals, and parents.

Let Us Know

After reading the book, SandCastle would like you to tell us your stories about reading. What is your favorite page? Was there something hard that you needed help with? Share the ups and downs of learning to read. We want to hear from you! To get posted on the Abdo Publishing Company Web site, send us email at:

sandcastle@abdopub.com

About SandCastle™

Nonfiction books for the beginning reader

- Basic concepts of phonics are incorporated with integrated language methods of reading instruction. Most words are short, and phrases, letter sounds, and word sounds are repeated.

- Readability is determined by the number of words in each sentence, the number of characters in each word, and word lists based on curriculum frameworks.

- Full-color photography reinforces word meanings and concepts.

- "Words I Can Read" list at the end of each book teaches basic elements of grammar, helps the reader recognize the words in the text, and builds vocabulary.

- Reading levels are indicated by the number of flags on the castle.

Note: Some pages in this book contain more than five words in order to more clearly convey the concept of the book.

Look for more SandCastle books in these three reading levels:

Level 1 (one flag)	**Level 2** (two flags)	**Level 3** (three flags)
Grades Pre-K to K 5 or fewer words per page	**Grades K to 1** 5 to 10 words per page	**Grades 1 to 2** 10 to 15 words per page

Elephants **are big.**

Some elephants live in zoos.

Many elephants **live in hot places.**

Elephants **have thick skin.**

Many elephants
have gray skin.

Elephants have large ears.

Elephants **eat grass.**

A baby elephant is
a calf.

Have you seen an elephant?

Words I Can Read

Nouns

A noun is a person, place, or thing

calf (KAF) p. 19
ears (IHRZ) p. 15
elephant (EL-uh-fuhnt) pp. 19, 21
elephants (EL-uh-fuhntss)
pp. 5, 7, 9, 11, 13, 15, 17
grass (GRASS) p. 17
places (PLAYSS-iz) p. 9
skin (SKIN) pp. 11, 13
zoos (ZOOZ) p. 7

Verbs

A verb is an action or being word

are (AR) p. 5
eat (EET) p. 17
have (HAV) pp. 11, 13, 15, 21
is (IZ) p. 19
live (LIV) pp. 7, 9
seen (SEEN) p. 21

More About Elephants
Match the Words to the Pictures

calf
ear
grass
trunk

24